OUT OF NORTH KOREA

A Korean Boy Tells His Rescue Story in Pictures

OUT OF NORTH KOREA

A Korean Boy Tells His Rescue Story in Pictures

with C. Hope Flinchbaugh and Jessica Austen

This book contains depictions of graphic violence not suitable for children.

HISTORY MAKER PUBLISHING

Honoring the Heroes in Our Family Tree

HISTORY MAKER
PUBLISHING

Honoring the Heroes in Our Family Tree

Out of North Korea
ISBN: 978-1-60066-274-4
LOC Control Number: 2010938629
Copyright © 2011 by History Maker Publishing, LLC

Printed in India
15 14 13 12 11   5 4 3 2 1

Lion artwork by Priscilla Williams. Used by permission.
www.living-water-productions.com
Cover Design by Pencil Tip Design.

This book contains the real-life experience of a child who was rescued miraculously out of North Korea. The names of the Chinese rescuer and the North Korean child she rescued are changed to protect them and their families from retaliation by Chinese and North Korean government authorities. This book contains depictions of graphic violence not suitable for children. If you would like to schedule a speaking engagement or interview or to order copies of this book or learn more about life inside North Korea, go to www.historymakerpublishing.com.

Dedication

To my parents and my older brother who are still in North Korea. I hope I will see you again one day. And to all the North Korean people—be safe. Do your best to survive until North Korea and South Korea are united into one Korea. Then we will experience ultimate freedom.

—Gil Su

Books by C. Hope Flinchbaugh

Fiction
I'll Cross the River
Across the China Sky
Daughter of China

Nonfiction
Out of North Korea
Spiritually Parenting Your Preschooler

Contact Hope at
www.historymakerpublishing.com

Acknowledgments

The first time I called Jennifer Garrido and explained my vision for this book, she immediately volunteered to take my children two days a week so that I could write. Jennifer, for the many hours invested in teaching, field trips and especially for your endearing friendship, thank you. You are a treasured and trustworthy friend.
                                                                                    Hope

To my amazing husband, Brandon—your sacrifices make my dreams possible. To Hope, for opening the door to pursue my passion to advocate for human rights and for guiding me in this adventure. I am forever grateful to you both.
                                                                                    Jessica

To my mother, Betty Keenan, for teaching me the power of "story" and supporting me as free-lance writer, author and now publisher. No one can tell a story like you, Mom!
                                                                                    Hope

Of course, this story could not be told without Gil Su, Mrs. Sao and their translator (who wishes not to be named here). All three have given History Maker Publishing their full written permission to publish this story in English, and we are deeply honored by their trust.

Thank you to the North Korea Freedom Coalition for putting this story into our hands and for tirelessly giving aid to and raising awareness of the Underground Railroad out of North Korea.

Thank you to Cleo June Sippel for freely offering her expertise in copyediting. The best is yet to come!

Jee Won Jeong, thank you for joining us "in the eleventh hour" to translate for Gil Su just before publication. Because of you, we were able to document the last-minute, critical updates to his mother's case in the North Korean prison camp. We're not giving up!

A special thanks to Sujin Park and Eun-Hye Kim from PSALT NK (www.psaltnk.org) of Englewood Cliffs, NJ, who willingly volunteered their skills in translating some picture captions written by Gil Su.

I am indebted to my cheerleaders, huddle buddies and dearest friends, Deborah, Jennifer, Carol and Bets. Can you feel this mountain tremble?
                                                                                    Hope

Contents

The Rescue

The following true story was told through a translator by Mrs. Sao, a Korean Chinese woman who lived in a city in China near the North Korea/China border. We have attempted to translate her story as closely as possible to her Korean words and expressions. Today Mrs. Sao (not her real name) lives in South Korea to evade capture and imprisonment by Chinese police for her "crime" of helping a Korean refugee boy and his family escape starvation in North Korea. Hiding North Koreans is considered a crime by the Chinese government and carries a heavy penalty. If caught, the North Korean refugee would be repatriated, and Mrs. Sao could be arrested, imprisoned and beaten. Mrs. Sao told her story...

The dream was simple, but it changed my life forever. It was August 21, 1999. A boy whom I never saw before squeezed my neck and yelled, "Please save me!"

I saw his young, round face clearly. He looked to be about fourteen years old, and he cried out again, "Please save me!"

"Boy, let go of my neck," I replied. "I feel like I'm being choked!"

"I will let go of your neck if you will save me," he said.

"Yes, I will save you!"

At that moment, the boy pulled his hands away, and I woke up. The clock said it was only three o'clock in the morning—it seemed so real, but it was just a dream.

I couldn't go back to sleep. The boy's face was still clear and vivid even after I woke up. I lay in the darkness and wondered who he was and why he'd asked me to save him. Maybe he lost his parents and could not find his way back home. I wondered, *What does this dream mean? Who is this boy?*

I lay awake for awhile, pondering the dream. At dawn I prepared breakfast for my sleeping children and husband and left a message on the counter:

Honey, I have something urgent. I have to go out now. Please have breakfast with the children without me.
Your wife

I wanted to know if my dream was real. I had a vague expectation that if I searched for this boy, I would find him. First, I went to the railroad station and searched for him from end to end. There was no one like him. I came out of the railroad station and walked on a wide, open road. In my head there was nothing but the face of this boy.

I said to myself, *I must find this boy. I must find him, buy him food, and if he is lost, I must find him his way back home.*

So I went to the airport, the bus terminal, the marketplace, anywhere I thought I could find him. I spent half the day looking for the boy, but there was nobody like him. This was ridiculous, really, because in a city of several hundred thousand people, how can you find a boy you never met but saw only in your dream? Suddenly I remembered the face of my friend—a sixty-year-old grandmother. I had my grocery stand next to hers at the same place in the market for about ten years. She had a stand of her own and sold newspapers, cigarettes, and other items. Once in a while I would have a dream, and whenever I told her my dreams, she always interpreted back to me what those dreams meant. So I went to the market to find her.

"What are you doing here?" she asked. "I heard you went to South Korea to make money. When did you come back?"

She was very happy to see me, but I was on a mission to find the boy in my dream. I said, "Well, Grandmom, let's talk about those things later. I have something urgent." I told her about my dream and the boy. In the end I asked her, "Have you seen a boy like the one in my dream?"

Grandmom answered, "Wait a while—he may show up here."

I sat next to her and watched the passersby very carefully, looking for the boy in my dream. Suddenly, a boy rode toward us on a bike. I realized immediately that the boy on the bicycle was the boy in my dream.

I stopped him on his bike, and the boy got startled and stepped back! I grabbed his hand. "Are you the one who came to my dream last night and squeezed my neck?" I asked.

The boy had a look of surprise on his face. The boy yelled, "Grandmom!"

Grandmom stood up and said to the boy, "Everything is okay. I know this lady very well. Don't be afraid."

The boy's eyes widened, and he stared at me. I looked at his face again very carefully—it was definitely the same face in my dream.

I wondered if he was lost on the street. Then I noticed—his neck had red marks, signs of a noose around his neck. I looked down. His wrists showed scars from handcuffs. That's when I knew. I asked the boy, "You crossed the river, didn't you? The Tumen River?"

The boy looked this way and that, and then he answered in a low voice, "Yes, I crossed the river."

I'd spent the last several months looking for Korean children who had narrowly escaped the starvation and death in North Korea by crossing the Tumen River into China. My friend Mr. Moon from South Korea had requested that I find North Korean children who had escaped from North Korea and ask them to draw pictures of their lives in North Korea.

I looked at my watch. It was 1:40 p.m. I asked him, "Did you have lunch?"

"No, I didn't have my lunch."

I took him to a restaurant nearby and bought him a bowl of cold noodles. And we talked.

"Why did you come to this city all by yourself?" I asked.

"No, I did not come by myself. I came with fifteen other people."

I was shocked. "What? Fifteen people? Where are they?"

The boy appeared nervous. "I cannot talk here." He stopped eating the cold noodles and began to cry.

"Okay, don't cry," I urged. "Finish your noodles, and we will go to a quiet place to talk."

His name was Gil Su. In January 1999, fourteen-year-old Gil Su escaped from North Korea by crossing the Tumen River with his aunt's family—his mother's sister's family. In July, his aunt was working at a Chinese restaurant and was arrested by the Chinese police and sent back to North Korea. (The Chinese government's policy is to repatriate any North Koreans hiding in China.) To save his aunt, Gil Su, his uncle and his cousin crossed the river and went back inside North Korea. North Korean police arrested Gil Su. He was taken to the National Security Bureau and tortured, interrogated and beaten up by security agents.

One night, he opened the windows of the small toilet and escaped. He hid at his relatives' house and escaped again to China. We met exactly one day after his second escape from North Korea. The fifteen people who crossed the river with him the first time were all his relatives, and they were hiding in various places: a construction site, a deserted house and other places. They slept in the streets.

I was happy to have found the boy in my dream, but I then realized I had fifteen people to take care of instead of one. My heart was heavy, and I didn't know what to do. So I called Mr. Moon in South Korea.

I asked Mr. Moon, "What should I do?"

Mr. Moon laughed and said, "What does it matter, one boy or fifteen people? I will come over right away, but in the meanwhile find a house where all of them can hide safely."

I wondered, *What does he mean? How can he protect all these people?* But I followed his instruction and found a house for them. For three years we hid Gil Su's family. We took them from one hiding place to another whenever necessary. We gave them food, clothing and shelter.

North Korea is a closed country—cameras are not allowed inside. Mr. Moon hoped that the children who escaped from North Korea would draw pictures from their pure perspectives of what they saw while living in North Korea.

While we were hiding Gil Su and his family, I asked Gil Su, "Can you draw?"

"Yes, I can," he answered.

I gave him crayons and paper. It is very fortunate that we can show the world what is happening in North Korea with these pictures.

Gil Su Illustrates His Story

While Gil Su hid in China, he spent his days drawing pictures of what life was like inside North Korea. Because the outside world is not permitted to take cameras into North Korea, Gil Su's pictures are valuable in helping us understand North Korean culture, lifestyle and government. Gil Su and his pictures are already famous in South Korea and Japan.

Yahoo, we have light! *

In North Korea, citizens have an average of one to two hours of electricity each day.
Electricity is generated by waterpower through a dam, and because there is not much
precipitation in North Korea, a full day of electricity is provided only on national
holidays, such as the birthday of Kim Jong-il or the birthday of his deceased father,
Kim il-Sung.

* *Note: Gil Su's handwritten captions and comments are italicized.*

Forced Haircuts

Cutting hair.

The government forced citizens to get haircuts so they could get foreign currency by selling our hair.

Hunger

I dream about food but wake up hungry.

세두리야, 네가 없었다면
칠 팔월 보리고개 어떻게
살았을가!

Se-Tu-Ri (Jang Gil-Su): This wild weed is the main food for North Koreans from early spring to late fall.

"세투리"(씀바귀의 함경북도 사투리)
이른 봄부터 늦가을까지 오늘날 북한 주민이 가장 많이 먹는 풀이라고 한다. 한 포기 풀잎을 통해 북한현실을 상징적으로 대변해 주고 있다.

Seturi, if we didn't have you, how were we supposed to survive through the "Bo-ri-go-gae"[bad harvest]!

이제는 모두가 초식동물이 [...]
언제면 이밥을 배불리 [...]

수 15살

We all became grass eaters.

Having little else to eat, North Koreans often strip leaves and bark
from trees, boil them, and eat them.

To survive means to eat anything that comes along.

20

You can't tell if this is pork or human flesh.
If you are not careful, you may end up eating boiled human leg.

The table of a government official's family.　　　　　*The table of a commoner's family.*

"Let's eat heartily today!"

The military gets special treatment. They eat while the citizens starve.

Sickness

Many people in North Korea contract grass poisoning from eating too much boiled grass. Grass poisoning is a rare disease that only a few animals have been known to get in isolated countries.

What should I do when there's nothing to boil? What do I eat tomorrow?

Stealing to Survive

I'll take my chances, even before a gun, if this is for food. . . .

"Stop!"

장마당에서 중국물건을 팔아 생계를 이어가는 그들을
뒤쫓아와 물건을 빼앗아내고 장을 보지못하게통제하다

총찬강도

Armed robbery.

In this picture, the North Korean policeman is actually robbing the lady. Gil Su gives us a twist on words here when he titles this "Armed Robbery," because police are supposed to be armed to protect the people, not steal from them.

Public Execution

Gil Su draws graphic pictures of an execution he saw as a child
in North Korea. A notice is posted: a man will be publicly executed for stealing
clothing, rice, and corn.

The North Korean police are ordered to kill to create a climate of terror.
Anyone who speaks against the "Dear Leader" Kim Jong-il will be executed.

Watching executions is mandatory. Any show of emotional sympathy toward the accused is seen as treason against the "Dear Leader."

Executions are often followed by mandatory shouts of loyalty to the Communist State such as:
"The great leader, comrade Kim Jong-il, is The Sun in the twenty-first century!"
"Long live the ideologically-sound state!"
"Long live the strong state!"
"Long live our own brand of socialism!"
"Praise Kim Jong-il!"
"Praise Father Kim-il Sung!"
"Praise him! Praise him!"

A person can be executed for the crime of singing a Japanese song, owning a Bible or, in this case, stealing food to feed his family.

Anyone caught trying to escape is either interrogated and put into an Auschwitz-style prison camp or gunned down.

No Pity for the Helpless

Three-year-old kotjebi.

"Kotjebi" is a name used as a slur against a child who is worse than homeless—
it means the child is parentless and roams around begging. Many adults in
North Korea have little pity for these orphans because they feel desperate to
find enough food to feed their own children.

Living in underground tunnel.

Children dig an underground tunnel under the bank of a small stream where they live all year long. These Kotjebi children arrange their living quarters so that the girls and youngest children lie in the inner part of the tunnel and the boys sleep near the front to guard the entrance.

Is this the human-centered society?

*We were repeatedly told that this is a human-centered society when we were
learning the Juche (self-reliance) theology. But these days the people are treated like
a fly. Nobody cares anymore that a person is dying on the streets.
There are no Good Samaritans there.*

A family in my village: they are all crying.

Mother said, "We are so pitiful that Mommy cannot feed your small stomach full. What good is it that we live? Let's jump to the river and drown ourselves."

Her child replied, "Mommy, I will never nag you to give me rice or food. Don't kill yourself."

Gil Su said this mother and her children were from his village. Sadly, all three plunged to their death as the mother said she could no longer cope with watching her children starve.

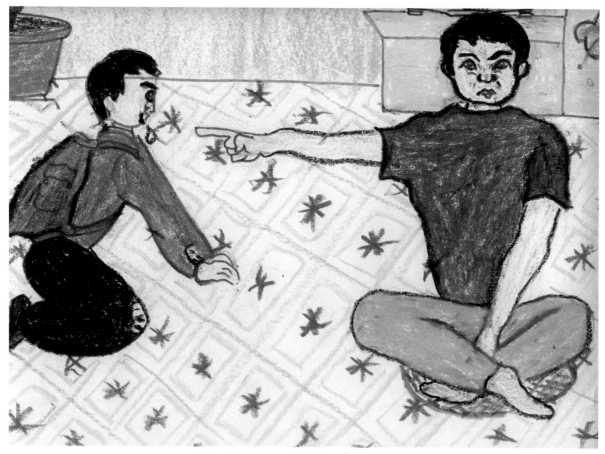

Desperate for food, Gil Su went to his uncle.

"Uncle, save us," I said. "I am here because I don't have anything to eat."
Uncle answered, "Last year you and I (uncle and nephew) got separated. This year
uncle and nephew have no connection anymore. Don't you know that next year
parents and son will be separate? Go away."
I lamented that because of food, father and son is no more a relationship, and the
uncle and nephew are nothing anymore because they have nothing to eat. Family
value is no more there because of deficiency of food.

Escape from North Korea

Border area.

This picture of the border area between North Korea and China is a picture of Gil Su's Promised Land, a place where he hopes to escape famine and fear and live a meaningful life with a full stomach.

Many obstacles stand in the way of leaving North Korea.

People who cross the river endanger their lives.

Captured

How could crossing Tumen River because of hunger be a crime?
This is the scene where I was caught by a North Korean guard.

Interrogation

Arrested, handcuffed and hit by North Korean guard.

"What crime did I commit?" I asked.
The officer replies, "You met a South Korean intelligence officer, didn't you?"
"No, I've never been to China," I answered. I denied it.

"Write a confession of your crime!"

I was forced to write the confession by a whip.
So I made up a story with a confession in it and gave it to the officer.

Escape!

"돼지를 주고 국경을 넘다"

중국에 도망쳤다가 형제들을 구하려고 다시 두만 강을 거너다 북한국경경비대에게 잡히다. 할머니 는 마지막 남은 전재산이나 다름없는 돼지 한 마 리를 경비대에 넘겨주고 나를 구출해 주었다.

After his escape from prison, Gil Su went to his grandmother for help.

Grandmother gives her pig to the North Korean officer to bribe him to allow me to cross the Tumen River. The pig was the only valuable property she owned.

Epilogue

Sadly, Gil Su's mother was arrested by Chinese police on March 6, 2001, and sent back to North Korea where she was put in a political prison camp. You will see her name included in the list at the back of this book of refugees and humanitarian workers seized and arrested in China. Gil Su learned that the North Korean government forced his parents to divorce after he and his mother tried to escape. Just before publication of this book, Gil Su heard that his mother, who is still in an Auschwitz-style labor camp, was recently coerced to sign a document that confessed to treason because she left North Korea—a document that indicts her for possible execution. This is not an unusual circumstance. Most defectors who are arrested and taken back to North Korea die from hard labor, starvation, torture, or execution in the prison camps.

In the end, there were fifteen people in Gil Su's extended family, including Gil Su, who successfully escaped North Korea to hide in China. Because it is difficult to hide a group of fifteen Koreans and because no one knew for sure who would make it to freedom in South Korea, the fifteen family members split up into three groups.

Seven members of Gil Su's family entered into the United Nations High Commissioner for Refugees (UNHCR) office in Beijing on June 26, 2001, and requested asylum to South Korea. It is rare that refugees are able to enter the UNHCR office in Beijing without being arrested by Chinese police. However, Mr. Moon timed it so that the refugees arrived when China wanted to announce the 2008 Olympics. Mr. Moon and others believe that Gil Su's family members were not detained long because China wanted to avoid an international incident at this time. The first group of seven family members arrived safely in South Korea on June 30, 2001. Three other family members traveled through another (undisclosed) country and arrived in South Korea on June 29.

Five other family members went to the Japanese Consulate in China on May 8, 2002. This is extremely difficult to do because the People's Republic of China provides their own police to "protect" all the embassies and consulates in China. This, of course, bars North Koreans from gaining access to the places that can protect them since Chinese police are ordered to arrest North Korean refugees. Therefore, the North Koreans remain stateless. With nowhere to turn for help, they go into hiding and hope to make it safely to South Korea before getting caught. Eventually, Gil Su's family traveled safely to South Korea, and news of their arrival was reported in South Korea, China, Japan, and the United States.

Gil Su is presently a student in North America.

Mrs. Sao's involvement in their rescue raised questions in her mind about God's involvement with the North Koreans. She said that she is not a

Christian but openly talks about her spiritual feelings. She told us, "What is God's miracle? When we do our best and something happens that we cannot comprehend, then that is a miracle. The Gil Su family of fifteen went to so many death traps, but they survived and got to be known in the world. They are very famous in Japan and South Korea. I think all of these are miracles. I risked myself many times between life and death, but I had no fear. Isn't it a miracle when someone is happy while risking one's own life to save other people?

"I don't know what God looks like. Is God a woman or a man? What does he look like? But if there is a God, truly what would he do when he sees all these terrible things happening in North Korea—starving to death, frozen to death, sick to death, and shot to death? Is he just standing by and watching them? Or is he going to rescue them, crossing the line between life and death all the time?

"Then I realized Mr. Moon was the man who God sent to this world to do his work. God does not have hands and legs like we do, so he needs someone to do his work in this world. I heard about Jesus Christ two thousand years ago; maybe he's the same kind of person. Maybe President Lincoln was the same kind of person God sent one hundred and some years ago. Mr. Moon knew what was happening in North Korea much earlier than anyone. He risked his life coming to China because Chinese police could have arrested him anytime. He laughed and cried with the refugees [this is a Korean expression of somebody going through 'thick and thin']. He is doing God's work.

"Mr. Moon mortgaged his parents' house, spent all his fortune, and sacrificed his own family to rescue North Koreans, to rescue his neighbors. This is something I could not understand before I got involved in his work. He may be a bad son to his parents, but he is someone who followed God's words—to save his neighbors and the people before he worries about his own household. People ask me now, 'Do you believe in God?' Then I answer them, 'I don't know God that I cannot see, but when I look at Mr. Moon ... if God comes here as a person, he would do the same as Mr. Moon does.'"

Note from C. Hope Flinchbaugh and Jessica Austen

As Harriett Tubman risked her life time and time again to help African Americans escape slavery in the South, in the same way Mrs. Sao and Mr. Moon and others continue to quietly assist North Koreans escape famine and Auschwitz-style prison camps in North Korea. (Yes, there are numerous reports of chemical experimentation within prison camps, including experimentation on families, including children, where scientists watch to see how long it will take a family to painfully die after eating chemically soaked cabbage or other such food.)

While the details of life inside of North Korea are gruesome, Gil Su's miraculous rescue after crossing the border the second time gives us great hope. If Gil Su experienced divine intervention through Mrs. Sao's dream and the compassion of his human family while attempting to escape, then we can believe that others can be rescued as well.

Today, people who look back at the events of the Holocaust often repeat the mantra, "Never again." In truth, a holocaust *is* happening again in the twenty-first century, and our human family is suffering unbelievable miseries. Why? So that a dictator who demands worship can be appeased. (Picture Stalin, Hitler, Mussolini, Mao.)

The question arises, "What can we do to help them when the government steals the international food aid they are given, and those who try to escape are so often seized by Chinese police and taken back into North Korea?"

Raise your voice.

Raise your voice.

That's it. Raise your voice.

Raise your voice in prayer.

Raise your voice in government.

Raise your voice in media.

Raise your voice until the "powers that be" decide to lay aside their politics, popularity polls, and bankrolls to rescue North Korean orphans **BECAUSE IT IS RIGHT**.

www.historymakerpublishing.com
Raise your voice. E-mail this website to your friends.

Seized by Chinese Authorities

The following is a list that the Defense Forum Foundation (DFF) began compiling in 2002 of the names of North Korean refugees and humanitarian workers who are known to have been seized by the Chinese authorities as a result of the People's Republic of China's refusal to abide by the international agreements it signed.

The current update to this list was conducted by Mr. Moon, Gil Su's rescuer; Sin U Nam of the International Coalition to Save North Korean Slaves; the staff of Free North Korea Radio in Seoul; and two American citizens who were jailed in China for rescuing North Korean refugees, Philip Buck, winner of the 2007 Civil Courage Award for his rescue of North Korean refugees, and Steve Kim, founder of 318 Partners.

Currently an average of one hundred to two hundred North Koreans *each week* are repatriated against their will by Chinese authorities to North Korea where they face torture, imprisonment and, increasingly, execution—**for the crime of leaving North Korea.** China's violent policy and its refusal to allow the United Nations High Commissioner for Refugees (UNHCR) and humanitarian organizations access to the refugees has led the North Koreans to become further victimized. Many end up as slaves, while 80 percent of female refugees become victims of sexual traffickers and are sold to brothels, Internet pornographers, or to Chinese men as "wives."

It is estimated that the rate of repatriations escalated in 2004 as part of China's campaign to end the refugee crisis in anticipation of the 2008 Beijing Olympics. However, China never stopped its campaign to send North Koreans back to North Korea.

This list represents only *a small fraction* of the number of North Koreans that have been repatriated against their will to North Korea. There are, of course, thousands and thousands of others who have been seized and forcibly repatriated to North Korea for which the dates and locations are not known to us.

Many people have contributed to this list over the years: American citizens who have been jailed in China for rescuing North Korean refugees, Steve Kim and Phillip Buck; Sin U Nam of the International Coalition to Save the North Korean Slaves; and the North Korea Freedom Coalition and its member organizations including Ana Jang and PSCORE, 318 Partners, Free the North Korean Gulag, and Kim Seung Min and the staff of Free North Korea Radio, the only defectors-based radio program broadcasting into North Korea.

A Note Regarding the Humanitarian Workers and China's Heinous Crime: Many of the humanitarian workers listed below were North

Korean defectors who had obtained South Korean citizenship but were forced back to North Korea. This makes China not only guilty of cruelty toward the refugees but also guilty of committing the same crime for which it has jailed humanitarians: illegally transporting people across the border. Except in this case, China is sending *legal citizens* of South Korea against their will to North Korea. No other government is committing this heinous act, other than North Korea, which already has a reputation for abducting citizens from other nations.

North Korea is officially called Democratic People's Republic of Korea and may be referred to as DPRK throughout this list.

THE LIST

Repatriated on 14 August 2010

5-year-old child (female), 70-year-old man, and others in their 20s and 30s (four males and nine females).

Repatriated on 3 August 2010

Two men (50s and 60s), eight females (20s and 30s). They were hiding in Dandong waiting to go to South Korea but were seized on 29 July. Three children (ages 5 and 6) were released but ten adults were repatriated.

Seized on 29 July 2010 and publicly executed after repatriation

Seven North Korean defectors, including ones from Shinuiju, were arrested by Chinese police in Dandong, China. Within a month, they were repatriated and executed in North Korea. Currently a female defector with South Korean nationality is being held in prison in Dandong.

Repatriated on 19 February 2010

Jung Sang-Woon (prisoner of war, male, 84), who was seized and jailed in China in August 2009, was sent to a political camp in North Korea. The Public Security Bureau (PSB) in China learned from a member of the North Korea National Security Agency who visited China to repatriate North Korean refugees that Mr. Jung had been sent directly to a prison camp as soon as he was repatriated. Before his escape, he had been living in North Korea for fifty years, forced to work as a miner since the Korean War.

Seized on 19 February 2010 near the border between China and North Korea

Lee, a defector correspondent for Free North Korea Radio (FNKR), was abducted by North Korea's security agents near the border between China and North Korea.

Repatriated in October 2009 to North Hamgyung, Onsung-gun

Forty-two people including children were repatriated during October. Twenty of them were investigated in Onsung-gun police agency.

Twelve Seized, ten repatriated in October 2009

Twelve North Korean defectors tried to escape from China to fly to Korea and the United States in Unnam province in China. However, a Chinese

Korean (Chosun-Jok) leaked information to Chinese authorities, and they were all caught. The Mission of Refugees sent a large amount of money so that two of them could be released, but the rest were sent back to North Korea.

POW family repatriated in September 2009

Two family members of a South Korean prisoner of war (POW) entered Shenyang's Korean consulate in mid-September but were repatriated. They were arrested while staying outside of the consulate due to "lack of facilities."

Seized in September 2009 near the Chinese-Vietnam border

- Na Young-Hyo (male, 50), from Chongjin, North Hamkyong Province, defected from North Korea in July 2009. His wife went missing in China during her attempt to flee to South Korea.
- Chon Hye-Son (female, 37) from Chongjin City, North Hamkyong Province, North Korea. A victim of human traffickers in October 2002, she is now traveling with her son, age 6, fathered by the Chinese man who "purchased" her from traffickers. Repatriated to North Korea in 2005, she defected to China for a second time in September 2008.
- Lee Chung-Kuk, Chon's son, born 9 February 2003.
- Chon Jong-Hwa (female, 43), originally from Musan, North Korea, defected to China on 17 March 2004. She is a former victim of human traffickers.
- Kim Wun-Nyo (female, 50), from Wonsan, North Korea. She defected from North Korea on 10 May 2009.

Seized 15 December 2008 in Jirin, China

Choi Young-Ae (female, 24), Yoon Eun-Sil (24, female)
Relatives of POW Mr. G, who has already resettled in South Korea.

Seized in September 2008 in Kunming Mountain area

Twelve North Korean refugees who were held in Dandong detention center and scheduled to be deported back to Sinuju, North Korea, on 28 November 2008. The oldest refugee was 48 years old, and there were also children. There was a North Korean spy arrested with this group who was believed to have posed as a refugee to thwart their escape.

Seized on 16 July 2008 in Yanji with the pastor who was sheltering her

Bahng Mi-Hwa (female, born 21 April 1972) in North Hamkyung Province

Seized on 21 April 2008 in Kunming

- Liu, Gil-Hwa (female, born 25 November 1966 in Musan)
- Lee Ae-Sook (female, born in 1982 in Musan)
- Yoon Geum-Hee (female, born 26 October 1979 in Hoeryong) and her 4-year-old daughter
- Sohn Ok-Joo (female, born 27 July 1991 in Saetbyeol)

Seized on 30 March 2008 on their way from Shenyang to Beijing (one hour from Beijing)

- Lee Soo-Kyeong (female, born in Cheong Jin City 5 October 1987)

- Kim Soon-Ok (female, born in Hwae Ryong City, 4 July 1967)
- Kim Joon-Sik (male, 26 years old, born in Hwae Ryong City)
- Kim Joon-Nam (male, 24 years old, born in Hway Ryong City, brother of Kim Joon-Sik)

Seized on 5 March 2008 in Shenyang, China

Hahn Chang Kuk (male, 30), Lee Jong-Sun (female), Lee Kung-Shin (female, 30) and Lee Jong-Shin (female, 33) were arrested by Chinese authorities and are now being held in Shenyang Border Patrol Detention Center.

Seized on 24 October 2007 in Yanji, Jilin Province, China

Lee Sang-Hyuk (male) and another North Korean refugee were seized by Chinese border police. Lee has already been jailed in North Korea for the crime of calling his South Korean relatives on a cell phone but escaped again to China.

Seized on 9 October 2007 in Beijing, China

Four North Korean defectors were seized at the South Korean International School. During this incident two South Korean diplomats were physically restrained by the Chinese police as they tried to prevent the arrest of the defectors.

Seized in August 2007 in Inner Mongolia

Yu Sang-Joon (male), a South Korean citizen, born in North Korea, was arrested by Chinese police while trying to help nine North Korean refugees escape to Mongolia.

Seized in June 2007 in Inner Mongolia

More than forty-four refugees were seized as they attempted to travel through Mongolia to get to South Korea.

Repatriated and publicly executed in 2006

Son, Jung Nam, former general of Korean People's Army, was repatriated and publicly executed. He was accused of meeting and passing information to his brother Jung Hun, who resettled in South Korea.

Seized in December 2006

The six refugees in jail in Shenyang include two orphan boys, ages 16 and 17; a 22-year-old woman; and three women in their 40s. One of the older women is the mother of a 19-year-old who made it to safety in the US Consulate and is awaiting resettlement in the United States along with two orphan boys. One of the women has relatives in Hawaii; another has family in South Korea.

Seized on 11 October 2006

Nine people from three families of POWs were repatriated:
- Kim, Yong Wha
- Lee, Jung Hha
- Lee, Jung Hoon
- And six others

Seized in March and August 2006

Lee, Yu Mi (female)

Repatriated on 20 December 2005

Kim, Geum Nam (male). After sixty days in Chinese prison, he was repatriated. He was interrogated and tortured for three hours one time while he was held at the Hyesan police agency. He was sent to a labor camp and stayed there for five days, but he was exempted from work due to his old age and severe frostbite.

Seized on 2 December 2005 from a Korean School in Beijing

Lee Chun-Sil had attempted to escape by entering a Korean school in Dalian on 30 November 2005 but was kicked out. She went to a Korean school in Beijing in December, but the Chinese police arrested her. Despite appeals by the South Korean and American governments, she was repatriated to North Korea sometime in the February/March 2006 time period.

Seized on 29 August 2005 from a South Korean school in Yantai, China

Two males and five females who entered the school during a ceremony were repatriated to North Korea on 29 September 2005 despite repeated requests and appeals by the South Korean government to allow them to travel to South Korea.

Seized in August 2005

Kim Song Sook (female, 27) was seized while attempting to cross the Mongolian border. Her younger sister escaped to South Korea.

Seized on 27 July 2005

These refugees were seized as they entered a Japanese residential quarter in Tianjin attempting to reach a Japanese international school:
- Kim Yong-Hi, mother (born 28 January 1962)
- Pae Wung, first son (born 4 November 1985)
- Pae Yong, second son (born 1 March 1995)
- Kang Song-Hee (born 5 February 1979)
- 51-year-old female (name unknown)

All of the above are believed to have been repatriated except for Kang Song-Hee, who was being detained in Tianjin. Because she has been repatriated twice already, it is feared that if she gets sent back again to North Korea she will face terrible torture, even execution.

Seized on 25 May 2005 in Chang Choon City

Two North Korean females, name and ages not known.

Seized on 22 May 2005 during a worship service in Chang Choon City

One North Korean male (26) and three North Korean females

Seized on 9 May 2005

These refugees were seized the same day that Pastor Phillip Buck was arrested. Buck was trying to help them get to Mongolia.
- Choi, Sang-Muk (male, 50)
- Han, Song-Hwa (female, 43)
- Kim, Pyung-Yong (male, 50)
- Park, Jeung-Lan (female, 45)
- Cho, Young-Sil (female, 43)
- Kim, Myung-Ok (female, 40)
- Kim, Hyung-Suk (male, 21)
- Han, Kum-Sook (female, 30)
- Choi, Soon-Kum (female, 60)

Seized in May 2005

- Kim Ryong-Chul (male, 26, Ham Heung City, South Ham Kyung Province)

- Kim Kyung-Sook (female, 25, On Sung, North Ham Kyung Province)
- Kim Keum-Sung (5 months old, born in Tsingtao, China)
- Kim Mo-Ran (female, 22, Chungjin City, North Ham Kyung Province)
- Male (name and age not known)
- Six to nine members of the Choi family (four of the people include: one male, two females, and a 5-year-old child, names not known)
- Kim Sung-Hee (female, 26, Moo San, North Ham Kyung Province)
- Kim Hyung-Hee (female, 15, Moo San, North Korea Province)
- "Sung Hee's mom?" (female, 50, Moo San, North Ham Kyung Province)
- Two males (names not known; traveled separately from Yanji)
- Two females (names not known; traveled separately from Yanji)

Seized in March 2005 in Longjing City in Jilin Province

Kang Gun ("Kang Sung-il," male, born 1969, Pyongyang) had become a South Korean citizen, but had traveled to China to get out information about conditions inside North Korea. He is credited with smuggling out footage of North Korea's infamous Yoduk prison camp that aired on Japanese television. He was reported as missing in Longjing City and believed to have been seized by North Korean agents in China and taken to Pyongyang. Because of his involvement in getting information out about North Korea's political prison camps, he is in grave danger of being tortured and executed.

He is reported to have been held in Pyongyang and then sent to a political prison camp.

Repatriated January 2005

Han, Man-Taek (POW, 73). He escaped from the North on 27 December 2005 but was seized the next day.

Seized between 2001-2005

These refugees were being sheltered by Phillip Buck. Their whereabouts are unknown.

Kim, Hyun Deuk (male, 55)
Han, Young Ae (female, 49)
Kim, Hae Young (female, 18)
Kim Chol Min (male, 16)
Kim Chol Joo (male, 14)
Han Eun Hee (female, 29)
Han, Seung Hee (female, 26)

Seized in early November 2004 from a hospital in Dandung, China

Lee Ju-Im (female, 73). Mrs. Lee is a South Korean citizen who was abducted to North Korea during the Korean War. She had escaped North Korea and was recuperating in a hospital when she was seized by North Korean security agents.

Seized on 25 October 2004

Fifteen North Korean refugees attempting to enter the Korean consulate office in China.

Seized on 25 October 2004 in the Tongzhou area of Beijing

Two humanitarian workers who had defected from North Korea and obtained South Korean citizenship and were rescuing other defectors:

- Lee Soo-Cheol (male, born 1963 in North Hamyoung Province). Lee was held for two years without trial and then sentenced to two years imprisonment in 2006.
- Kim Hong-Gyun (male, born 1965 in South Hamgyoung Province). Kim was held for two years without trial and then sentenced to five years imprisonment in 2006.

These rescuers were seized in a surprise raid at 3:00 a.m. along with more than sixty North Korean refugees who were hiding in two shelters, including eleven children and a 70-year-old man. The refugees include:

- Kim Soon-Ok (female, 25, from Eundok), who defected to China approximately seven years ago and who has two children ages five and two years old.
- Kim Soon-Bok (female, 33, from Eundok), who defected to China approximately seven years ago and who has one child, three years old.
- Kim Kyung-Ok (27, from Eundok), who defected to China approximately seven years ago.

It has been reported that sixty-two of these refugees were repatriated to North Korea on 9 November 2004.

Seized shortly after the October 2004 incident in Shenyang

Hong Jin-Hee (male, born 1969 in Hamyeung), a North Korean defector who had obtained South Korean citizenship and was involved in rescuing other North Koreans from China. He had managed to escape the surprise raid but was tracked down and arrested in Shenyang. He was detained for two years without trial and then sentenced to seven years imprisonment in 2006.

Seized on 27 September 2004

Nine North Korean refugee women and children at the Shanghai American School in Shanghai, China. Two children were released to South Korean officials, but the other seven women and teenagers are still being held.

Seized on 8 August 2004 in Podung, China

Jin Kyung-Sook (born 24 June 1980), a North Korean defector who had established South Korean citizenship in 2002, was forcibly seized by North Korean agents and repatriated to North Korea.

Seized July 2004 in Yenji

Oh Young-Sun (male, born 1965), a North Korean defector who had obtained South Korean citizenship, went to China to make a documentary about the Changbai Mountains. While he was in China, he met up with North Korean refugees and helped them escape to South Korea. Later, while he was filming Baekdu Mountain, he was arrested and tried in 2005 for the crime of helping North Korean refugees to escape to South Korea. He was given an eight-year prison sentence.

Seized sometime between 5 and 10 June 2004 in Nanning, China

Yun Hyang-Shim (female, born 12 January 1956), who had defected from North Korea and is now a South Korean citizen. She was caught trying to help her son-in-law escape to Vietnam and is being held in Nanji Prison in Nanning City.

Seized on 15 February 2004 in Nanning, Guangxi Province

Kang Eun-Hee (25), Park Il-Man (38) and five other North Korean refugees were seized by Chinese authorities and sent to Ansan Refugee Camp in Tumen, Jilin Province on 5 March 2004. After going on a hunger strike to try to gain their freedom and safe passage to South Korea, they were repatriated to North Korea on 12 March 2004. They are reported to have been sent to Onsong Political Prison Camp.

Seized on 23 December 2003 while attempting to travel to Beijing, China

Choi Song-Juk (mother of Lyu Myung-Ho and Lyu Sung-Ho—see 18-19 September 2001 entry).

Seized on 13 December 2003 in Guangxi

Three Japanese-born North Korean refugees: Choi Yong (male, 60) born in Hiroshima; a man in his 50s born in West Japan; and Shin Chung-Mee (female, 46) born in Tokai Region, Japan.

Seized on 5 December 2003 in Nanning City

Chinese authorities seized thirty-six North Korean refugees hiding in Nanning City, Kwangzi Province.

Seized on 26 September 2003 in Guangdong Province

The following refugees were seized when 54-year-old New York businessman Steve Kim was trying to help them. Kim served four years of a five-year prison sentence in China, while the two Chinese women assisting him served two years in prison for helping these refugees:

- Choi Keum-Chun (male, 19)
- Park Young-Chul (male, 19)
- Park Hang-Chul (male, 52)
- Chung Song-Hee (female, 12)
- Park Kyung-Sook (female, 38, mother of Chung Song-hee)
- Chung Hwa-Keum (female, 36)
- Kim Il-Hwa (female, 36)
- Song Yeun-Hee (female, 40)
- Park Choon-Hee (female, 40)

Seized in early September 2003 in Yunnan Province

Nine of these refugees were arrested by Laos Police while trying to cross the Laos border. They were repatriated to China and then to North Korea. Two of the refugees eventually escaped to South Korea with the help of Pastor Buck:

- Yun Jong-Ok (female, 37)
- Yun Kwang-Chol (male, 34)
- Park (first name not known, female, 31)
- Lee So-Bong (female, 54)
- Ko Kum-Suk (female, 34)
- Ko Hye-Suk (female, 32)
- Ko I-Song (female, 27)
- Ko Song-Hi (female, 24)
- Oh In-Sun (female, 20)
- Ko Jong-Hi (female, 40)
- Oh In-Chol (male, 15)
- Oh Jong-Hwa (female, 34)
- Kim So-Hi (female, 27)
- Sohn Mi-Hyang (female, 8)
- Chung Hye-Yong (female, 26)
- Kwak Hyon-Chol (male, 21)
- Kim Kwang-Il (male, 18)

- Park Kum-Song (male, 18)
- Ye Song-Jin (male, 20)
- Chang Chol (male, 19)
- Dong Chong-Shil (male, 19)
- Kim Mi-Na (female, 16)
- Kim Un-Hye (female, 17)
- Yu Song (female, 15)

Seized on 5 September 2003 in Guangzhou

Dr. Woo Ri-Chae, a North Korean biological weapons expert, was seized while trying to enter the Australian consulate general office in Guangzhou. Dr. Woo's wife and children fled when he was seized.

Seized on 18 August 2003 at Pingxiang, China, near the Vietnam border

- Choi Soon-Hwa (female, 56)
- Song Jung-Hwa (female, 22)
- Lee Kwang-Rim (male, 23)
- Han Kwang-Suk (male, 14)
- Han Eun-Byul (female, 12)
- Moon Kwang-Hyuk (male, 22)

Seized on 7 August 2003 in Shanghai

These refugees were seized along with Japanese humanitarian worker Fumiaki Yamada, who was later released:

- Chang Gyung-Chul (male, born 22 September 1969)
- Chang Gyung-Soo (male, born 21 March 1972)
- Chang Mi-Hwa (female, born 15 January 1969)

The two brothers and their female cousin were repatriated to North Korea. The two brothers are believed to be in the North Korean State Security Agency Detention Center in North Hamgyung Province.

Seized on 1 August 2003 at the train station in Beijing

These refugees were on their way to the South Korean Embassy when they were seized. Rev. Jung and Rev. Pak, who were assisting in their rescue, were jailed for a year and a half for helping them. All six refugees were repatriated to North Korea six months later:

- Mr. and Mrs. Lee
- Mr. Park
- Mr. and Mrs. Kang and their daughter

Seized on 27 July 2003 in Beijing

These four were arrested outside a restaurant in Beijing. On the day of their arrest, they had arrived from the city of Yanji by the Tumen-Beijing express train.

- Lee Kil-Wun (male, 64, coal mine administrator from the Onsong district, North Korea)
- Han Sun-Bok (female, 60, wife of Mr. Lee Kil-Wun, former high school teacher, from the same district)
- Lee Song-Min (male, 31, son of Mr. Lee and Mrs. Han, worker, from the same district)
- Kang Myong-Ok (female, 35, from the city of Chongjin, North Korea)

Seized on 27 July 2003 in Quingdao, China

Eight North Korean refugees including four children

Seized in April 2003, somewhere in China

Newlyweds Kim Cheol-Hoon (born 1970 in Hwanghae Province) and Shin Sung-Shim (born 1981 in North Hamgyeong) were defectors that had become South Korean citizens. They were seized in

China and abducted to North Korea while on their honeymoon.

Seized April 2003 in Changbai China

Kim Chul-Soo (born 1965) and Ji Man-Gil (born 1971) were both from Hyesan, Yanggang Province, but had become South Korean citizens. According to Kim's wife and Ji's brother, the two traveled to China to try to rescue their family members, including children from North Korea, but were abducted by North Korean refugees to North Korea.

Seized on 18 January 2003 in Yantai City, Shandong Province

- Park Yong-Chol (male), a North Korean national. On 22 May 2003, sentenced to a two-year imprisonment and a fine of 5,000 RMB. Believed to have been forcibly repatriated to North Korea in October 2004.
- Park Yong-Ho (in Chinese, "Piao LONGGAO"), male, an ethnic Korean Chinese national. On 22 May 2003, sentenced to a three-year imprisonment and a fine of 10,000 RMB.
- Ko Chong-Mi (female, born 23 September 1960 in Japan Osaka Ikunoku Tennoji)
- Lee Yu-Son (female, born 21 September 1982 in Pyon an Puk Do, DPRK)
- Kim Son-Hee (female, born 1 September 1961 in Han Gyong Puk Do, Kil Ju Gun Yong Buk Ku, DPRK)
- Pee Okk-Ju (female, born 11 February 1988 in Han Gyong Puk Do, DPRK)
- Kim Myong-Chol (male, born 28 January 1965 in Han Gyong Puk Do, Rajing Jang Pyong Dong, DPRK)

- Chu Hun-Kuk (male, born 29 December 1956 in Han Gyong Puk Do, Kil Ju Gun Yong Buk Ku, DPRK)
- Kim Yong-Ho (male, born 17 December 1969 in Han Gyong Puk Do, Fe Ryong City, Yok Chon Dong, DPRK)
- Kim Kum-Ok (female, born 28 March 1960 in Han Gyong Nam Do, Ham Hung Song Chon, DPRK)
- Sin Young-Hee (female, born 14 July 1986 in Han Gyong Puk Do, Seppyor Gun An Won Li, DPRK)
- Choun Hyang-Hwa (female, born 10 July 1983 in Han Gyong Nam Do, Ham Hung Song Chon Kang Yok John Dong, DPRK)
- Kim Un-Kum (female, born 25 June 1931 in Han Gyong Puk Do, Myon Chon Kun, DPRK)
- Be Kwang Myong (male, born 1 January 1986 in Han Gyong Puk Do, Chong Jin Chong, DPRK)
- Park Ran-Hee (female, born 17 January 1964 in Han Gyong Nam Do, Ham Hung Yong Song Gu Yoku, DPRK)
- Lee Kyong-Su (male, born 18 February 1968 in Yang Kang Do, He San City, DPRK)
- Lee Chol-Ho (male, born 28 August 1967 in Han Gyong Puk Do, Chong Jin City, Chong Jin, DPRK)
- Lee Chol-Nam (male, born 26 April 1969 in Han Gyong Puk Do, Chong Jin City, Chong Jin, DPRK)
- JangYong-Chol (male, born 20 April 1955 in Han Gyong Puk Do, Chong Jin City, Chong Jin, DPRK)

Seized on 13 November 2002 at the Vietnam/China border

These seventeen refugees were seized by Vietnamese border guards and turned over to Chinese authorities. After their arrest they were held in Pingshang, Nanying City, Guangxi Province, China.

- Kim Ok-Ryun (female, 38)
- Kim Myung-Hee (female, 33)
- Choi Kil-Sook (female, 62)
- Kim Kum-Dan (female, 67)
- Hwa Jung (age 28)
- Lee Sung-Yeol (male, 20)
- Kim Chul-Ho (male, 44)
- Lee Hwa-Jun (male, 35)
- Park Yoon-Sang (male, 54)
- Cho Kyung-Sook (female, 29)
- Cho Sung-Sook (age 26)
- Kwak Myung-Neo (male, 35)
- Yoon Seo-Young (female, 24)
- Chun Chang-Sup (male, 42)
- Hwang Tae-Wook (male, 9)
- Oh Song-Wol (age 4)
- Lee Dae-Ho (7 months old)

Seized on 31 October 2002 at the German School in Beijing
- Joo Seung-Hee (female, 41, Hamkyung Bukdo)
- Han Mee-Kyung (female, 17, daughter of Joo Seung-Hee)
- Lee Sun-Hee (female, 39, Hamkyung Bukdo)
- Kim Ok-Byul (female, 14, daughter of Lee Sun-Hee)
- Kim Kwang-Soo (male, 16, son of Lee Sun-Hee)

Seized on 30 October 2002 in Dalian
Kim Gun-Nam (male)

Seized on 2 September 2002 at the Ecuadorian Embassy in Beijing
- Han Song-Hwa (female, 45)
- Cho Seong-Hee (female, 16, daughter of Han Song-Hwa)

- Cho Hyun-Hee (female, 12, daughter of Han Song-Hwa)
- Kim Yeon-Hee (female, 31)
- Cho Il-Hyun (female, 10 months, daughter of Kim Yeon-Hee)
- Choi Jin-Hee (female, 28)
- Chung Kwon (male, 28)
- Cho Young-Ho (male, 20)

Seized on 31 August 2002 near the Mongolian border
Yun Kim-Shil (female)

Seized on 26 August 2002 at the Chinese Foreign Ministry in Beijing
These seven refugees (known as "The MoFA Seven") attempted to apply for asylum at the Chinese Ministry of Foreign Affairs:
- Kim Jae-Gon (male, born 1942, from Kowun Kun, Hamkyong Nam-Doh Province)
- Kim Jong-Nam (male, born 29 August 1967, from Hwae-Ryung City, Hamkyong Buk-Doh Province)
- Kim Mi-Young (female, born 1970, from Un-San Kun, Pyong-An Buk-Doh Province)
- Jo Song-Hye (female, born 25 February 1976, from Dan-Chun City, Hankyoung Nam-Doh Province)
- An Choi-Su (male, born 20 March 1963, from Hungnam Ku, Hamkyong Nam-Doh Province)
- Ko Dae-Chang (male, born 4 September 1949, from Pyongyang)
- Kim Hong (female, born 12 April 1973, from Pyongyang)

Seized between 24 and 26 May 2002 in Yunnan Province near the Laos/Burma/China borders

Six North Korean defectors of which three names are known:
- Lee Song-Yong (male, 3.) His mother, Park Sun-Hi, female, 31, defected successfully to South Korea in 2000.
- Lee Hong-Gang (male, 48)
- Kim Mi-Hwa (female, 30)

Seized on 20 May 2002 in Yanji, Jilin Province

Kim Kyung-Il (male, born 17 January 1976). Mr. Kim is in Changchun Tiebi Prison serving a twelve-year prison term for the charge of helping North Koreans escape from China.

Seized on 10 May 2002 while attempting to reach Thailand

- Kim Chul-Soo (male, 63)
- Kim's wife (female, 60)
- Kim's daughter (female, 30)
- Choi Soon-Kum (female, 59)
- Kim Myung-Wol (female, 45)
- Pack Nam-Gil (male, 18)
- Park Myung-Chul (male, 45)
- Han Young-Ae (female, 45)
- Han's husband (male, 47)
- Eun Shim (female, 10)
- Eun Shim's brother (male, 14)

Seized on 12 April 2002 in Yanji, China

These two refugees were seized along with Rev. Choi Bong-Il, who was sentenced to nine years imprisonment when he was caught helping these refugees:

- Shin Chul (age 24)
- Choi Sung-Gil (age 23), repatriated to North Korea but escaped again and is now in South Korea

Seized 29–30 December 2001 near the Mongolia border

These refugees were seized trying to cross the China/Mongolia border near the border town of Dongchi in northeastern Inner Mongolia when Pastor Chun Ki-Won was arrested. Pastor Chun served eight months in a Chinese prison for trying to help these refugees. Two other refugees in the group who had U.S. relatives were allowed to go to Seoul. After their arrest, these refugees were held at Manchu-Ri Prison in China:

- Roh Myung-Ok (female, 38, wife of a South Korean citizen Chung, Jae-Song)
- Chung (Jung) Yoon (Eun)-Mee (female, 10, daughter of Roh Myung-Ok)
- Chung (Jung) Yoon (Eun)-Chul (male, 8, son of Roh Myung-Ok)
- Kim Kwang-Il (male, 32)
- Kim Chul-Nam (male, son of Kim Kwang-Il)
- Kim Ji-Sung (male)
- Nam Choon-Mee (female, wife of Kim Ji-Sung)

Seized 18–19 September 2001 in Yanji

These brothers are believed to be at Changchun Tiebei prison serving a five-year prison sentence:
- Lyu Myung-Ho (male, born 9 July 1977)
- Lyu Sung-Ho (male, born 8 September 1979)

Seized on 11 June 2001 from shelters established by Christian nongovernmental organizations (NGOs) in Xian, Shaanxi Province

Fifty North Korean defectors including the following:

- Choi, Kum-Chul (male, born 10 December 1958); currently in prison at Changchun Tiebei Prison; sentenced to twelve years in prison for helping North Koreans escape from China.
- Cho, Chul-Sok (male, 28, from Hamhung, Hamnam); currently in prison at Hoeryung (camp #22) Political Prison Camp.
- Jung Yong-Chol (male, 42, from Onsong. Hambuk); currently in prison at Hoeryung (camp #22) Political Prison Camp.
- Lee Kil-Su (male, from Wonsan, Kanwon); currently in prison at Hoeryung (camp #22) Political Prison Camp.

During this time period, two surviving female North Korean defectors also reported that Kim Ju-Bok (male, 26) was seized in Dandong and repatriated to North Korea where he was sentenced to death for leading a group of North Korea defectors. Among his group were six defectors who were sentenced to fifteen years imprisonment, and seventeen defectors who were sentenced to ten years imprisonment in Yodok Political Prison Camp.

Seized on 6 March 2001 in Yunkil, Jilin Province, China

Jung Soon-Ae (female, born 5 February 1955), **the mother of Gil Su**, seized by Chinese police and repatriated to North Korea on 13 March 2001. On 15 April 2001 she was taken to a prison in North Korea. Jung Soon-Ae was recently coerced to sign a document that confessed treason because she left North Korea—a document that indicts her for possible execution. Gil Su specifically requested that her name be added to "The List" because "raising her name may keep her alive."

Seized on 16 September 2000 at their "safe house" in Dalian by Chinese police

- Han Won-Chae (male, 60)
- Shin Keum-Hyun (female, 58)

Their son, Han Sin-Hyuk, was not captured and successfully defected to South Korea.

Seized on 17 January 2000 by North Korean security agents in China

Rev. Kim Dong-Sik (male, born 10 October 1947). Rev. Kim is a citizen of South Korea but also has a US Green Card. He is believed to have been abducted to North Korea, and recent testimony by a North Korean spy who was involved in his kidnapping confirms this suspicion. His wife and children live in Chicago.

Seized in Russia in November 1999

These defectors received refugee status from UNHCR, but Russia forcibly returned the refugees to China on 30 December 1999. China then forcibly returned the refugees to North Korea on 12 January 2000. One of these refugees escaped again to South Korea.

- Kwang Ho Kim (male, 23)
- Ho-Won Chang (male, 24)
- Young-Il Ho (male, 30)
- Young-Sil Bang (female, 26, wife of Mr. Ho)
- Woon-Chul Kim (male, 20)

- Dong-Myung Lee (male, 22)
- Sung-Il Kim (male, 13) was released due to being a minor.

Seized on 6 August 1997 by Chinese police in Jian, Liaoning Province

Li Song-Nam (age 51)

Seized on 4 February 1997 at the Shanghai International Airport

Kim Eun-Chol (male, 35). Kim's parents (Kim Jae-Won and his wife) live in South Korea and believe he was sent back to North Korea.

Seized on 7 July 1995 in China

Rev. Ahn Seung-Woon, a citizen of South Korea, was last seen in Pyongyang.

Also Note This Brave Rescuer:
Disappeared January 2005

Jeffrey Bahk, US citizen and resident of Georgia, disappeared crossing the Mekong River in January 2005 while helping six North Korea refugees escape. The six refugees made it to South Korea, but no one knows what happened to Bahk. It was reported that he drowned while others claimed he was in jail in Kenpun, Burma. South Korean officials reported that they visited Kenpun, and he was not there. His wife and other family members have been trying to find out what happened to him.

FORMERLY ON THE LIST

The following are defectors that were once on this list but made it to safety.

Repatriated in 2007 and 2008 but escaped to freedom in South Korea

Choi Myung-Sin (female)

Repatriated in 2007 but escaped to freedom in South Korea

Song Jae-Im (female)

Repatriated in 2006 but escaped to freedom in South Korea

Lee Yu-Mi (female)

Repatriated twice in 1998 and 2006, but made it to South Korea in the end

Kim Sun-Sook (female)

Repatriated in 2005 but escaped to freedom in South Korea

Kim Geum-Nam (male)
Park In-Sook (female)
An Hye-Young (female)

Repatriated in 2004 and 2005 but escaped to freedom in South Korea

Sin Hyang-Sook (female)

Repatriated in 2003, 2004 and 2005 but escaped to freedom in South Korea

Na Deok-Jin (male), underwent fifteen day of investigation and "pigeon" torture

Repatriated in 2003 and 2005 but escaped to freedom in South Korea

Yoon Boon-Ryun (female)

Repatriated in 2002 and 2005 but escaped to freedom in South Korea

Um Choon-Sil (female)

Repatriated in 2004 but escaped to freedom in South Korea

Seo Eun-Chan (female)
Lee Ok-Sook (female)

Seized in 2003 but escaped to freedom in South Korea

- Yang Yong-Ho (male, born 30 March 1961 in Han Gyong Puk Do, mu san gun, DPRK)
- Yang Gum-Soon (female born 2 December 1987 in Han Gyong Puk Do, mu san gun, DPRK)
- Kim Young-Kwang (male, 20 years old, born in DPRK)

Seized in 2003 but escaped to freedom in Japan

Chiba Yomiko (alias) (female, born 23 September 1960 in Japan Osaka Ikunoku Tennoji)

Seized in early September 2003 in Yunan Province

These refugees escaped again in 2004 and made it to South Korea with help of Pastor Phillip Buck:
Kim Kwang-Il (male, 18)
Park Kum-Song (male, 18)

Repatriated in 2002 but escaped to freedom in South Korea

Lee Young-Ok (female) and her son (14)

Seized on 12 April 2002 in Yanji, China

Choi Sung-Gil (23) was repatriated to North Korea but escaped again and is now in South Korea. She was seized with Rev. Choi Bong-Il, who was sentenced to nine years imprisonment.

Repatriated in 2001 and 2002 but escaped to freedom in South Korea

Lee Bok-Soon (female)

Repatriated in 1997 but escaped to freedom in South Korea

Kim Dong-Nam (male)

The following are humanitarian workers who were formerly in jail and were part of THE LIST but happily have been taken off due to their release

USA Citizens

Seized on 9 May 2005

Pastor Phillip Jun Buck (American citizen since 1989, resident of Washington state, born 6 January 1941 in North Korea) was held in Yanji for the crime of helping North Korean refugees. He had been in Chungdao City and had left with three American pastors to travel to Yanji via Beijing. All four were seized by Chinese police, but the three other American pastors were released. Buck was considered "a big fish," and he was held for a year and a half until his trial on 30 December 2005. The verdict was announced in 2006 deporting him on 19

August 2006. He received the 2007 Civil Courage Award from the Train Foundation for "steadfast resistance to evil at great personal risk." He is credited with rescuing over one hundred refugees until his arrest.

Seized on 26 September 2003 in Guangdong Province

Steve Kim, (Kim Seung-Whan, born 1949), an American businessman sentenced on 5 April 2004 to five years in jail, deportation and a 20,000 RMB fine for helping North Korean refugees. He was held in Yanji prison, Chan Chung prison, and the prison in Beijing. He was released 25 September 2007, one year earlier due to credits he earned as a prison laborer. He is credited with rescuing over one hundred refugees until his arrest.

Seized 27 July 2003

Rev. Park Young-Hwa, an American citizen, was held for a year and a half for helping North Korea refugees. He was seized on 27 July 2003, officially arrested on 8 September 2004 and released in late October 2004.

Seized on 12 April 2002 in Yanji, China

Rev. Choi Bong-Il (54), humanitarian worker caught helping two North Korean refugees and sentenced to nine years imprisonment. He was released on 22 September 2004.

South Korean Citizens

Seized on August 2007 in Inner Mongolia

Yu Sang-Joon (male), a South Korean citizen (born in the DPRK), was arrested by Chinese police while trying to help nine North Korean refugees escape to Mongolia. He was released in November 2007.

Seized on 18 January 2003 in Yantai City, Shandong Province

Choi Yong-Hun (male), a South Korean humanitarian aid worker. On 22 May 2003, he was sentenced to five years imprisonment and a fine of 30,000 RMB. He was subjected to torture and beatings during his imprisonment and was released early on 29 November 2006. It is believed he was released early because of his weakened mental and physical health caused by the abuse he endured in prison.

Seized on 31 August 2002 in Changchun in Northeast China

Kim Hee-Tae, humanitarian worker, was seized along with eight North Korean refugees attempting to leave China. He was sentenced to seven years imprisonment but was released on 15 July 2004.

Seized between 29–30 December 2001 near the Mongolia border

Pastor Chun Ki-Won, a human rights activist, was held from December 2001 until August 2002 (220 days in jail) for trying to help a group of North Korean defectors reach Mongolia.

Japanese Citizens

Seized on 7 August 2003 in Shanghai

Fumiaki Yamada, humanitarian worker with Society to Help Returnees to North Korea and a citizen of Japan, was seized with North Korean refugees he was trying to help. He was released after one week.

Seized on 13 December 2003 in Guangxi

Takayuki Noguchi (male, 32), humanitarian worker with Life Funds for North Korean Refugees, seized by Chinese police along with three Japanese-born North Korean refugees he was trying to bring safely to the country of their birth. Noguchi was released in August 2004 after nine months of incarceration.

Seized from his hotel room in November 2002

Hiroshi Kato, humanitarian worker with Life Funds for North Korea Refugees and a citizen of Japan, was seized at his hotel in China for helping North Korean refugees and held in prison for one week in November 2002.

Chinese Citizens

Korean-Chinese, who helped defectors, was seized and sent to the North in April 2008

Lee, Gi-Cheon (42), a broker for defectors, guided defectors to Yenji province from the border. He was seized by North Korean security agents near the Tumen River.

Seized on 27 September 2003

Lee Bok-Ja (female, 51), arrested by Chinese Border Police, served a two-year sentence for providing transportation to four North Korean refugees from her church in Yanji to Changchun City as part of a rescue operation with Steve Kim.

Lee Young-Ok (female, 46), the wife of a church pastor, arrested by Chinese Border Police, served a two-year sentence for buying tickets for four North Korean refugees so they could travel from Chang Chun to Guang Zhou in southern China as part of a rescue operation with Steve Kim.

Both women spent part of their sentence (eleven months) in the same prison with Steve Kim.

Seized on 22 May 2003

Park Yong-Ho (male), an ethnic Korean Chinese national, was sentenced to three years imprisonment and a fine of 10,000 RMB.

Seized on 18 January 2003 in Yantai City, Shandong Province

Kim Song-Man (Chinese version, "Jin CHENGWAN"), ethnic Korean-Chinese national, sentenced to one year imprisonment and a fine of 1,000 RMB. Kim served his sentence and is now free.

Many more Chinese citizens have been imprisoned and are in jail today, but we do not know their names, only that they helped rescue refugees.

Why the List?

Can reading these names actually save a life? Yes! Three different people who were victims of trafficking while attempting to escape North Korea were overwhelmed with grief because their daughters, too, were victims of sex trafficking. There seemed to be no way to find their daughters and no way to get out of the trap of sex trafficking. While contemplating suicide as the only way out of the horrible trap, they heard on the Chinese shortwave radio that people in the United States were protesting on their behalf, and their names were being read in front of the Chinese Embassy in Washington, DC. With renewed strength that others were with them, they escaped from China, and these three different people approached Suzanne Scholte, chairperson of the Defense Forum Foundation (DFF), with their individual stories. One Korean man heard his name read over the radio and was greatly relieved to know he was not forgotten. Another man who volunteered to help North Korean refugees in China was arrested and beaten. Someone smuggled a radio into his prison cell and while he was listening to Radio Free Asia, he heard his name called out loud at a protest in front of the Chinese Embassy. He was encouraged that others knew of his plight and was eventually released from prison. He was so moved that he actually flew to the United States and stood in front of the Chinese Embassy and participated in reading the names himself!

The purposes of the previous list are:

1. To raise our voice for justice to the government of China, because it is responsible for the fate of everyone listed on these pages.
2. To keep the names before us always so that we will not forget their imprisonment and their suffering.
3. To allow this list to be used by human rights organizations to help them join us in advocating for the release of all these individuals whether they are currently in Chinese or North Korean political prison camps.

This list was compiled in cooperation with seven nongovernmental organizations (NGOs) working with the DFF to rescue North Korean refugees. The list was compiled by DFF's chairperson, Suzanne Scholte, and reviewed for accuracy by the Seoul-based Citizens Coalition for Human Rights of Abductees and North Korean Refugees, the Japan-based Life Funds for North Korean Refugees, Abraham H. Lee of Refugee Phan, James Butterworth and Lisa Sleeth of Incite Productions, and several others who need to remain anonymous. The list has been periodically submitted to the People's Republic of China (PRC) along with letters requesting release of the individuals still in their custody and information

about the whereabouts of those who have disappeared. The list has been read aloud at many
protest rallies around the world including several held at the PRC Embassy in Washington, DC,
the PRC Embassy in Prague, Czech Republic, and
the PRC Embassy in Warsaw, Poland. It has been
submitted as part of testimony given by DFF to
the US House Committee on Foreign Affairs,
the US Congressional Executive Commission on
China, and the US Commission on International
Religious Freedom.

How Can I Help?

1. Tell someone that you care what happens to North Korean citizens, especially the children now hiding from Chinese police.

2. Link your website to www.historymakerpublishing.com

3. Pass this book to a friend.

4. Help North Korean orphans. Each time you purchase a copy of this book, you've donated money to finance safe houses and initiate rescues of North Korean orphans through the Underground Railroad.

5. Purchase a copy of this book and send it to your senator and/or congressman. Tell them that you care about what happens to these children. Suggest that our government appeals to China to set up adoptions of the stateless North Korean orphans. American families have successfully adopted Chinese children for years. Our government can ask China to allow us to set up legal adoptions of North Korean orphans who are hiding inside China. Why not?

6. Spread the word. Coauthor Jessica Austen is available for speaking engagements or interviews. Please contact her through www.historymakerpublishing.com.

7. If you would like to understand more about what goes on inside North Korea, read Hope Flinchbaugh's novel *I'll Cross the River*. This novel brings the reader into the mind-set of a brainwashed, starving North Korean who courageously takes her baby and small son across the river into China.

8. If you'd like more information on how you can help, contact the publisher at www.historymakerpublishing.com

If you would like to see more pictures by Gil Su,
visit www.historymakerpublishing.com.

Cowardice asks the question: Is it safe?

Expediency asks the question: Is it politic?

Vanity asks the question: Is it popular?

But conscience asks the question: Is it right?

And there comes a time when one must take a position

that is neither safe,

nor politic, nor popular;

but one must take it because it is right.

REV. DR. MARTIN LUTHER KING, JR.

It's time.

A portion of the proceeds from this book will go to finance safe houses and initiate rescues of North Korean orphans through the Underground Railroad. If you are interested in more information about this effort, please contact the publisher at www.historymakerpublishing.com.

Honoring the Heroes in Our Family Tree